FUTUREWORLD

TOMORROW'S TECHNOLOGY TODAY

JOEL LEVY

SCHOLASTIC

CONTENTS

INTRODUCTION

The seeds of the future are here in the present. Today, in laboratories and factories, in computer simulations and on drawing boards, a huge range of mind-blowing technology is taking shape. Right now, someone is testing a flying motorcycle or a revolutionary material to turn your clothes into solar cells. Lab technicians are growing replacement body parts for a patient, while others are fitting someone with a bionic foot. A researcher is discovering how much faster than the speed of sound a magnetically levitating train will travel. Another scientist is connecting a computer to someone's brain so they can control a robotic arm in the next room by thought alone.

What's more, according to some **futurists** (people who try to predict the future), new technologies and inventions will arrive faster and faster as the pace of change accelerates. The next 50–60 years will see more technological progress than the previous 20,000 years combined.

But **FUTUREWORLD** is not science fiction. It's about the near future, not the far future.

While it covers projects that are being planned now but won't be completed until the far future, such as asteroid mining, this book mostly predicts developments that are likely to come to fruition over the next 15–25 years.

There are good reasons for not looking too far ahead. As the Nobel Prize-winning nuclear physicist Niels Bohr once said, "Prediction is very difficult, especially about the future." Many previous attempts to predict the future have turned out to be wrong.

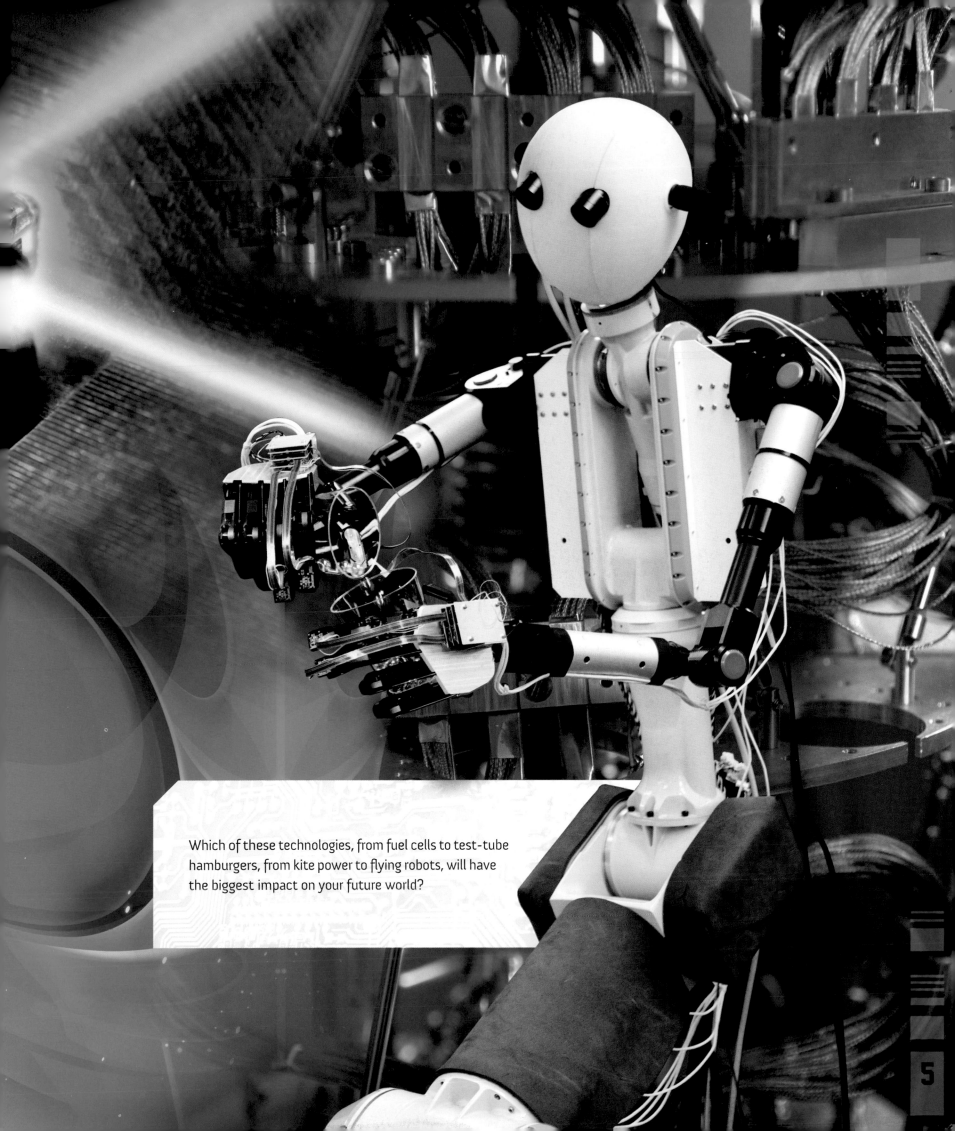

Which of these technologies, from fuel cells to test-tube hamburgers, from kite power to flying robots, will have the biggest impact on your future world?

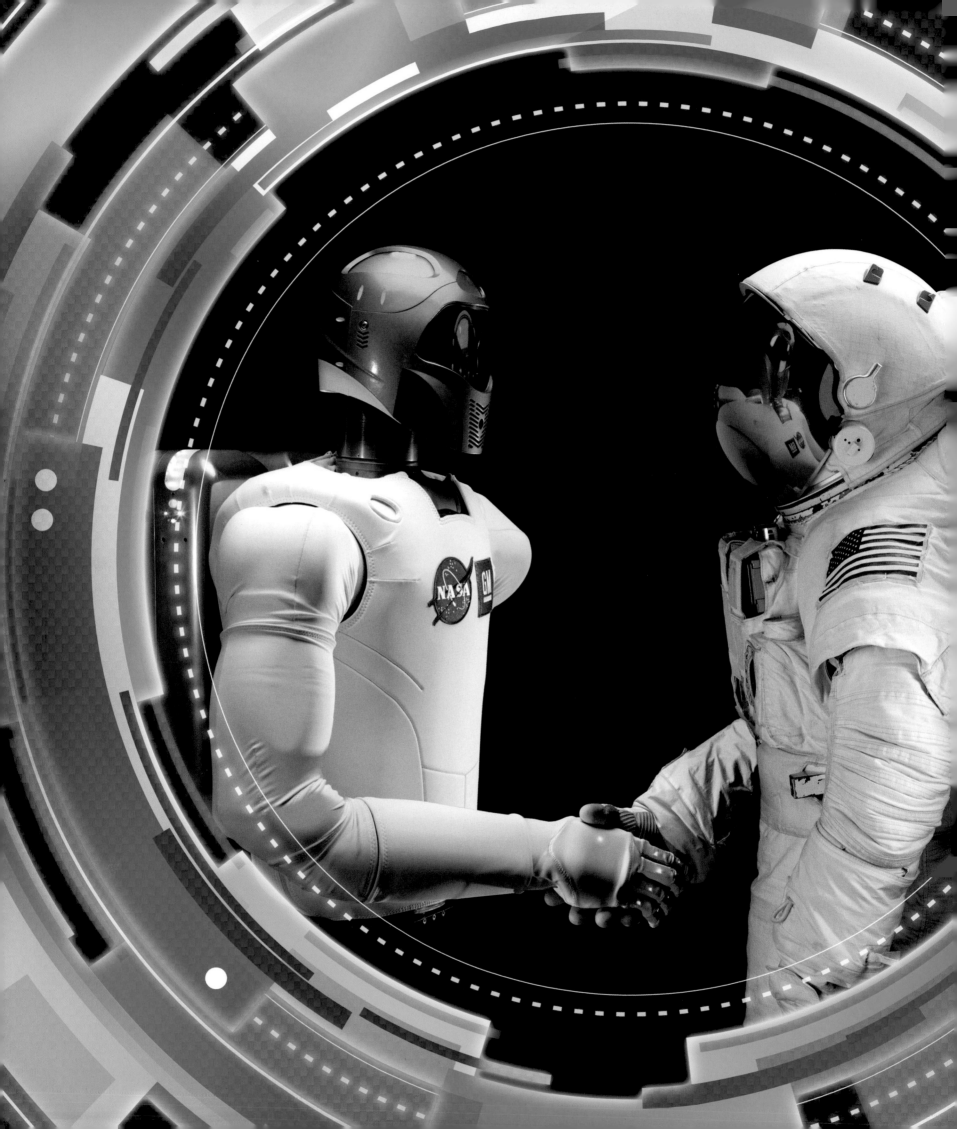

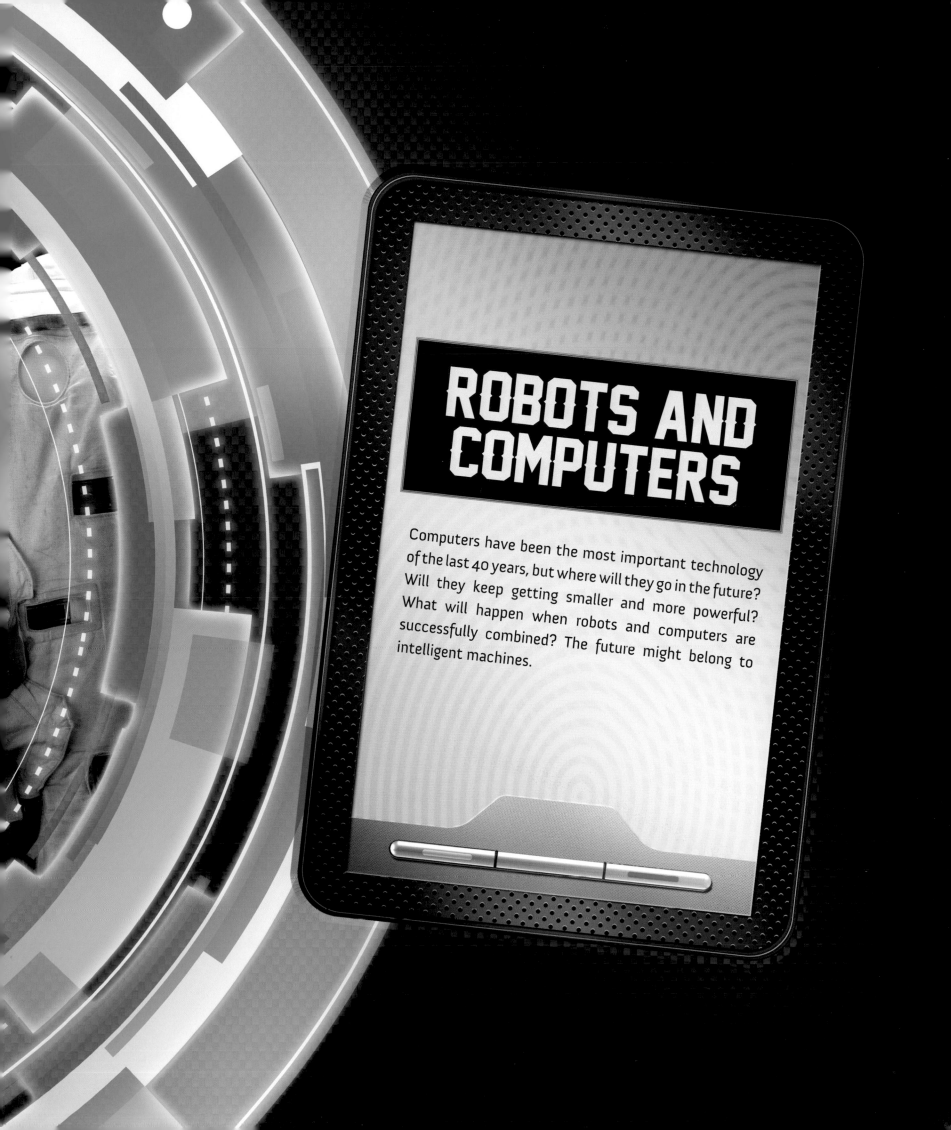

ROBOTS AND COMPUTERS

Computers have been the most important technology of the last 40 years, but where will they go in the future? Will they keep getting smaller and more powerful? What will happen when robots and computers are successfully combined? The future might belong to intelligent machines.

VIRTUALLY THERE
TELEPRESENCE

Telepresence ("distant presence") means being able to interact with faraway people and objects as if they were right here. Today's technology uses video screens that turn or move around a little. In the near future, it may be possible to remotely inhabit a robot that can walk, talk, touch, and feel. Controlling a robot from a distance is called **telerobotics**.

THE CURIOSITY ROVER IS REMOTELY CONTROLLED FROM EARTH AS IT EXPLORES MARS.

ABOVE..
A JAPANESE EMERGENCY ROBOT DESIGNED TO WORK IN DANGEROUS PLACES.

GET CONNECTED

The main driving force behind the coming telepresence revolution is **bandwidth**—the amount of information that is carried by a communication channel, such as a **fiber-optic** cable or radio signal.

In the recent past, the bandwidth available to individuals was only enough for voice calls, but it will soon be possible for anyone with a cell phone/internet connection to send and receive high-quality 3-D images.

Robotic tools are becoming cheaper. Mobile cradles for smartphones are already available. The screen showing your face can turn around and even move from room to room. In the near future, your video presence will be able to walk around and pick things up, thanks to telerobotic technology.

BELOW..
A RESEARCHER TESTS A ROBOTIC ARM CONTROLLED BY BRAIN WAVES.

INTELLIGENT MACHINES
ARTIFICIAL INTELLIGENCE

Artificial intelligence (AI) is the ability of a machine to think and not just follow a program. At the moment, machines can be programmed to do quite complex jobs, but only within limits. Tasks that humans find simple, such as navigating a crowded room or telling the difference between a weed and a flower, are too difficult for robots—so far.

AI IN OUR TIME

Films like *The Terminator*, *The Matrix,* and *2001: A Space Odyssey* feature intelligent machines that have taken control. In real life, however, AI cannot pilot spaceships or plot against humanity.

Real-world examples of AI include:

- computer programs that write simple newspaper articles
- programs that control trillions of dollars of business deals without any help from humans
- the Curiosity rover that is exploring Mars, which uses a very limited form of AI to help it get around without banging into things or tipping over
- Robonaut 2 (see right), which is in use on the **International Space Station**.

ALL-SEEING EYES

If computer programs could be made intelligent enough to see like we do, computers could take over all sorts of important but boring and difficult jobs. In the next ten years, expect to see computers looking for criminals by spotting their faces on CCTV video surveillance, or watching out for forest fires and dangerous weather events.

ABOVE....................
THE MACGYVER PROJECT
IS WORKING ON A RESCUE
ROBOT FOR DISASTER
SITUATIONS.

RIGHT...........................
ROBONAUT 2 IS DESIGNED
TO WORK IN SPACE,
USING THE SAME TOOLS
AS HUMANS.

FARMER BOTS

Farming is a field where AI could make a big difference. If tractors could be fitted with farming AI they would become farmer bots, able to tell the difference between weeds and crops. Weeds could be killed with tiny dots of pesticide or even blasted with mini-flamethrowers, while crop plants could be given water.

ABOVE...

ROBOTS FROM HARVEST AUTOMATION LOOK AFTER PLANTS ALMOST AS WELL AS HUMAN WORKERS.

POWER SUITS
EXOSKELETONS AND CARING ROBOTS

Exoskeleton means "outside skeleton." Animals like crabs and insects have exoskeletons. Thanks to exciting new technology, humans benefit from exoskeletal "**power suits**" that boost the wearer's strength and endurance.

EARLY PROTOTYPES

Early exoskeletons were too heavy and had to be plugged in for power.

EXOSKELETONS TODAY

Carbon fiber composites and advanced batteries make exoskeletons available now. For instance, the HAL robotic suit from Cyberdyne (left) can be used by emergency rescue teams, giving them the extra power to move debris and lift injured people. NASA is developing the X1 exoskeleton for astronauts to wear, so that they can move heavy objects in space.

LEFT..

THE HAL SUIT GIVES EMERGENCY RESCUE WORKERS EXTRA LIFTING POWER.

RIGHT...

THE X1 ROBOTIC EXOSKELETON WILL HELP ASTRONAUTS MOVE OBJECTS IN SPACE.

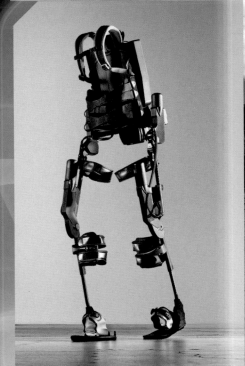

ABOVE AND RIGHT............
THE EKSO SUIT ENABLES
PEOPLE WITH PARALYZED
LEGS TO WALK.

SUPERPOWERS FOR EVERYONE

In the near future, advanced exoskeletons will help soldiers to carry heavy loads, and make it easier for nurses to lift patients. For the disabled, exoskeletons will help paralyzed people to walk.

CARING ROBOTS

Caring robots are robotic nurses and companions that help with day-to-day tasks.

Caring robots are already available. ROBOHELPER helps people get out of bed. The Robovie carries purchases. Toyota's Human Support Robot picks up objects and relays video calls. In the near future robot pets will provide companionship for elderly people, while at the same time monitoring health and helping around the house.

SQUEEZABLE CIRCUITRY
THE COMPUTERS OF TOMORROW

The first computers were giant machines that filled entire rooms and took a whole day to do a single calculation. Today a small games console packs as much power as a 1997 supercomputer.

MOORE'S LAW

Since the late 1970s, computers have followed a rule set out by leading computer engineer Gordon Moore. He predicted that the number of **transistors** crammed onto a single **chip** would double every two years. More transistors equals more computing power. Moore was saying that computers would double in power every two years. Amazingly, he was right. In 1969, the computer that guided the Apollo spaceship to the Moon had around 17,000 transistors; today your desktop computer has up to 14 billion transistors on a single chip.

So will computers in 2025 be 64 times as powerful as they were in 2013? Possibly. Breakthroughs with carbon nanotubes (a form of **nanotechnology**) suggest that Moore's Law will hold true for a while longer.

QUANTUM COMPUTING

According to **quantum physics**, some **subatomic particles** can be in more than one place at the same time. They can carry out more than one calculation at a time. If crystal-based computers could harness this ability, they could become thousands of times more powerful.

BELOW.............................

THE MOTOROLA HC-1 IS A
HANDS-FREE COMPUTER
THAT RESPONDS TO VOICE
COMMANDS.

ABOVE...

HANDS-FREE TABLETS ARE CURRENTLY UNDER
DEVELOPMENT, USING EYE-TRACKING TECHNOLOGY.

COMPUTERS YOU CAN SQUEEZE

The touchscreen is already replacing the keyboard, and voice and gesture control of computers are also available. These will become more widespread, as will other ways of communicating with your computer.

Foldable screens will become available, and it will be possible to make a computer out of almost any material.

BELOW...

WITH SANDSCAPE YOU COULD SHAPE AN OBJECT
FROM SAND AND SEE IT APPEAR ON SCREEN.

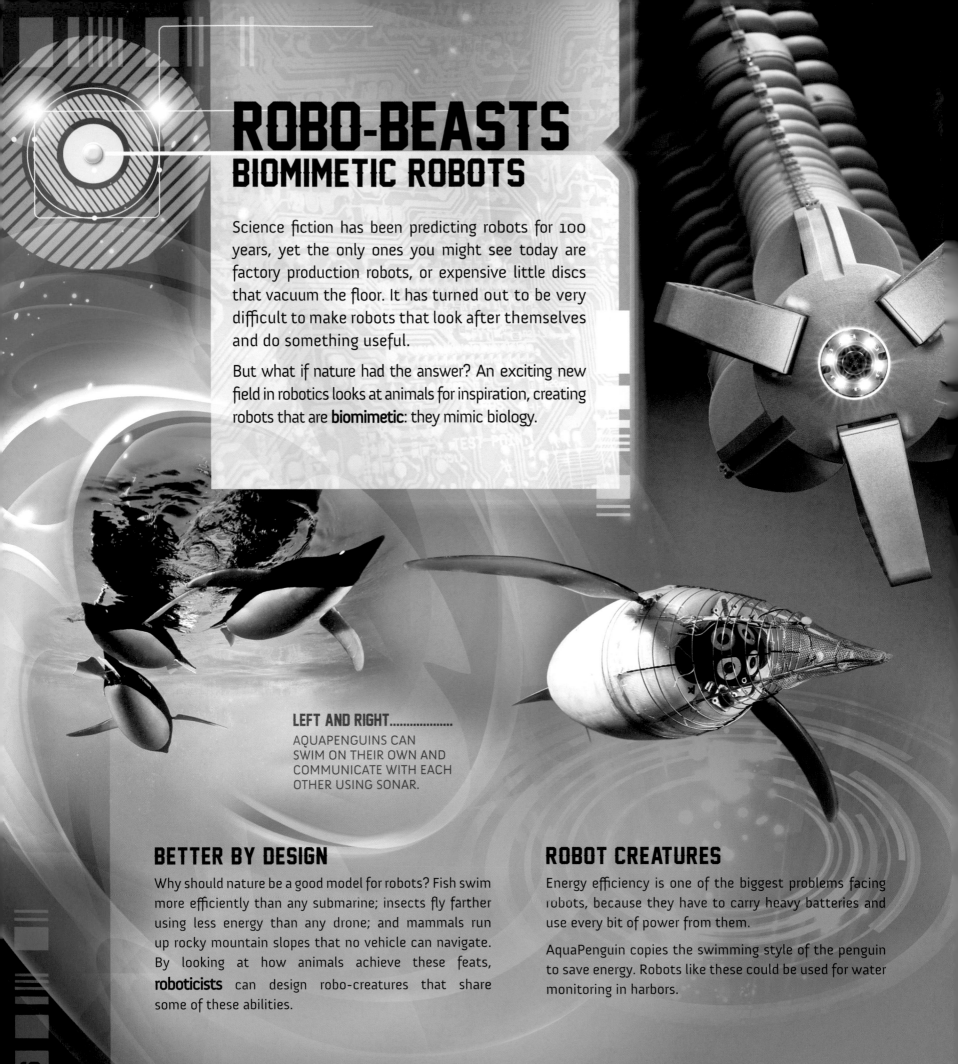

ROBO-BEASTS
BIOMIMETIC ROBOTS

Science fiction has been predicting robots for 100 years, yet the only ones you might see today are factory production robots, or expensive little discs that vacuum the floor. It has turned out to be very difficult to make robots that look after themselves and do something useful.

But what if nature had the answer? An exciting new field in robotics looks at animals for inspiration, creating robots that are **biomimetic**: they mimic biology.

LEFT AND RIGHT..................
AQUAPENGUINS CAN SWIM ON THEIR OWN AND COMMUNICATE WITH EACH OTHER USING SONAR.

BETTER BY DESIGN

Why should nature be a good model for robots? Fish swim more efficiently than any submarine; insects fly farther using less energy than any drone; and mammals run up rocky mountain slopes that no vehicle can navigate. By looking at how animals achieve these feats, **roboticists** can design robo-creatures that share some of these abilities.

ROBOT CREATURES

Energy efficiency is one of the biggest problems facing robots, because they have to carry heavy batteries and use every bit of power from them.

AquaPenguin copies the swimming style of the penguin to save energy. Robots like these could be used for water monitoring in harbors.

BIG DOG

Big Dog, developed for the U.S. military, copies animals like dogs and buffalo. It moves fast on slopes and rocky ground, is difficult to knock over, and gets up if it falls over. Robots like this could act as packhorses, or help mountain rescue units carry injured climbers.

ABOVE....................................
THE FESTO BIONIC HANDLING ASSISTANT MIMICS AN ELEPHANT'S TRUNK.

RIGHT....................................
RESEARCH GROUP DARPA IS DEVELOPING PACK ROBOTS THAT CAN CARRY KIT FOR SOLDIERS.

BELOW....................................
THE FESTO SMARTBIRD FLIES IN THE SAME WAY AS A HERRING GULL DOES.

FLIGHT AND SPEED

Robotic bees and dragonflies need little energy for flying because they are very light. By flying in the same way as their insect inspirations, they hover, land, and take off vertically and are highly maneuverable. Such robo-critters could be used for surveillance, or to explore damaged buildings.

RIGHT....................................
ANOTHER DARPA ROBOT, THE CHEETAH, CAN RUN AT 46.6 MPH.

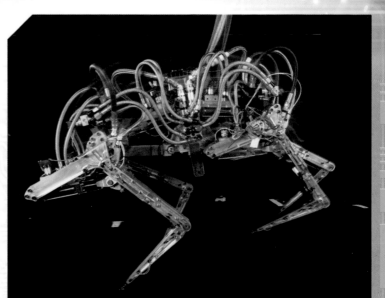

SHOPPING AND LIFESTYLE

The greatest impact of technology for most people comes in their day-to-day lives, in ways that are often almost invisible. Did you know that many of the things you buy today—even clothes and food—contain tiny microchips that talk to computer control systems?

This section explores how everyday life could change in the near future. Learn how your smartphone will run your life and disappear at the same time; how your fridge will order your groceries for you; and how your friends could leave digital graffiti visible only to you.

SMART MONEY
FUTURE SHOPPING

Ten years from now, shopping will be very different. As you walk past a store it will offer you a special deal on exactly what you want. You will walk in, pick up the goods, and walk out without going through checkout or handing over any money.

SMART SHOPPING

The internet has already caused big changes in shopping. There are very few record stores anymore because music is increasingly downloaded online. Smartphones are also beginning to affect the way people shop. It is now common for shoppers to find an item they like in a physical store and then use their smartphone to see if it is cheaper online or somewhere else.

BELOW..
SMARTPHONES COULD SOON BE THE STANDARD WAY TO PAY FOR A MEAL IN A RESTAURANT.

LEFT................................
THE STYLEME ELECTRONIC MIRROR
MAKES TRYING ON CLOTHES IN A
STORE EASY.

VIRTUAL REFLECTIONS

Visible technology will include virtual mirrors, which show you not just your reflection but also what you look like wearing the clothes you picked. While you look in the mirror, a shopping assistant robot will hold your bag.

NEAR-FIELD COMMUNICATION

Many items now carry microchips called **radio frequency identification** (RFID) tags, which are able to broadcast simple information about an item, such as its serial number and price. These tags can be monitored by scanners and by some new smartphones.

Over the next five to ten years, RFID technology will be replaced with a similar but more advanced version called **near-field communication** (NFC). With RFID, tags signal to smartphones, but the "conversation" is one-way. In NFC, the conversation is two-way; slightly more advanced versions of RFID tags give items, advertisements, and even walls, counters, bags, and boxes the ability to "talk" to your smartphone. They can exchange information if the phone and the tag are within 4 inches (10cm) of one another.

Eventually shopping trips will involve simply walking into the store, picking up whatever you want, and leaving. The payment will be automatically taken out of your bank account.

LEFT...
RFID CHIPS ARE MANUFACTURED
BY PRINTING THEM ONTO FOIL.

A NEW WAY OF SEEING

AUGMENTED REALITY

If you look online at a picture of the Colosseum, an amphitheater in Rome, you can see notes, links to extra information, and even re-creations of what it used to look like.

Imagine if you could see all of these things while actually in the Colosseum. When you look at the ruined floor of the arena, you could see gladiators battling against a crowded backdrop. Thanks to augmented reality (AR), this is already possible.

RIGHT...................................
IMAGINE VISITING A DINOSAUR THEME PARK! WEARING AR GLASSES, YOU COULD WALK AROUND THE PARK AND SEE IMAGES OF EXTINCT CREATURES, ALONG WITH TEXT INFORMATION.

SMART EYEGLASSES AND HUDS

Augmented reality is information and/or images electronically added to the real world, which you can see in real time at real locations.

Right now you can see AR by looking at a scene through a smartphone or tablet, but Google's Project Glass smart eyeglasses showcase technology that will soon become widespread. These devices contain computers that project info and visuals onto the lenses of the eyeglasses, which are transparent enough to see the real world.

LEFT...................................
GOOGLE'S SMART EYEGLASSES CONTAIN A COMPUTER THAT PROJECTS DATA ONTO THE LENS.

DIGITAL GRAFFITI AND VIRTUAL FAMILIARS

Almost every aspect of life could be touched by AR. You could look at an advertisement and directions to the relevant store would pop up. If a friend wanted to warn you that a restaurant had bad food, she could leave **digital graffiti**: a virtual message embedded in cyberspace, which you would see in AR when you looked at the restaurant.

You could generate virtual characters, creatures, and scenes that you would encounter through AR. You could be accompanied by your own virtual **"familiar"**— imagine a small dragon that only you could see, which acts as a digital assistant.

AUGMENTED INFORMATION

AR is already used in tourism. Imagine how exciting historical sites would be if you could see a re-creation virtually overlaid on the scene, or if you could look at a skeleton in a museum and see a virtual re-creation of the animal superimposed on it.

In school or college, AR could add background information to a picture posted by the teacher, or let you look up answers on the internet with just a glance.

BELOW..
AR ALLOWS A TOURIST TO WALK DOWN A STREET AND SEE IMAGES OF HOW IT USED TO BE ON HIS IPAD.

Tyrannosaurus rex
A fearsome predator that walked the Earth 66 million years ago.

SUPERCOMPUTER IN YOUR POCKET
FUTURE SMARTPHONES

The smartphone in your pocket is already more powerful than a desktop computer from two or three years ago. If you use a computer in school or at work, you probably sit at a desk with a desktop computer or a laptop.

SMALLER AND BETTER

The actual processing part of the computer may have shrunk to pocket-size, but there is no substitute for a proper keyboard and a decent-sized screen.

All that may be about to change.

THE SMARTPHONE WILL SOON BE SET FREE TO TAKE OVER YOUR DIGITAL LIFE.

DEVICE CONVERGENCE

Smartphones already have the processing power to handle documents, play video, and surf the Net. They already display something called **device convergence**. This is where jobs that used to need different devices can all be done by a single device.

Previously you needed a camera to take pictures and a CD player to play music. Now your smartphone includes a phone, camera, computer, stereo, Web browser, and navigation. Nissan has developed an app that allows a smartphone to drive a car. There are apps for controlling your home, checking your health, and listening for restless babies. Soon smartphones will take over the jobs of credit card and wallet (see page 20), door and car keys, passport, travel passes, and airline tickets.

ENTER THE PDA

It will be more accurate to describe your smartphone as a **personal digital assistant** (PDA). What's more, the PDA device could play host to a virtual assistant, an artificial intelligence that anticipates your needs and does routine tasks for you, such as booking flights or "talking" to your fridge to see if it needs to order milk. Google's Now and Apple's Siri are primitive versions of this.

THE MEMOTO LIFEBLOGGING CAMERA IS A FORERUNNER OF THE ALWAYS-ON PDA. IT TAKES TWO PHOTOS A MINUTE, CREATING A COMPLETE RECORD OF THE WEARER'S PAST.

LEFT....................................
NOKIA IS DEVELOPING THE MORPH, A BENDY SMARTPHONE THAT YOU CAN WEAR AROUND YOUR WRIST.

EVOLVING PDAS

What about the need for screens and keyboards? Using near-field communication (see page 20), advanced wireless technology, and harnessing the processing muscle of cloud-based computing, your PDA will wirelessly plug into whatever devices are nearby. Since almost any surface in the house, school, or car will double as a screen, there will be no shortage of screens available. You won't need a keyboard or mouse because you will be able to control the PDA by voice or gesture.

25

Miniaturization, cloud-based computing power, and new materials mean your future smartphone could look like almost anything, or even flit from item to item, "possessing" whatever is nearby.

INTELLIGENT LIVING
SMART HOMES

Over the next decade, technology will save you energy, take care of all the boring jobs, make you comfortable, and educate you. Digital technology will be built into the fabric of houses, so that computers can control every aspect of the home and talk to you wherever you are.

Using printable foodstuffs such as lab-grown meat proteins, your food printer will be able to create everything from burgers and burritos to weird and wonderful new taste sensations.

ELECTRICITY EVERYWHERE

Buildings of the future won't have wall sockets. You will soon be able to charge phones, robots, and other technology without wires. To save energy, computers controlling appliances will automatically turn off anything that is not in use.

Your smart home will welcome guests and block intruders by using **biometric scanning** to confirm identity. It will be able to read your face, understand your voice commands, and recognize your gestures.

Your smart home might spot that you are feeling gloomy and choose one of your favorite songs to cheer you up, routing it to speakers around the house so that the sound follows you wherever you go.

ABOVE.............................
THE DIGITAL CHOCOLATIER CREATES CUSTOM CHOCOLATES.

RIGHT...........................
THE CORNELL FOOD PRINTER LETS YOU PRINT FOOD IN ANY SHAPE.

STICKYBOT, A GECKO-INSPIRED CLIMBING ROBOT. THE HOUSE CLEANER OF THE FUTURE?

BELOW...

THIS AMAZING FUTURISTIC FRIDGE STORES AND COOLS FOOD BY SUSPENDING IT IN **BIOPOLYMER** GEL

ROBOT REVOLUTION

Robots will sneak into your future home, but they won't be the androids from the movies. Small and slow, these robots will quietly putter around in the background, doing the housework. Some will be able to climb walls or fly around, so they can reach the corners. They will stay out of your way.

GLASS CONTROLS

Touch-sensitive glass will soon be a major feature of your home. For example, one interactive screen could allow you to control all the appliances in your kitchen.

BELOW...........................

THE HOUSE OF THE FUTURE WILL HAVE A KITCHEN RANGE MADE OF INTERACTIVE GLASS.

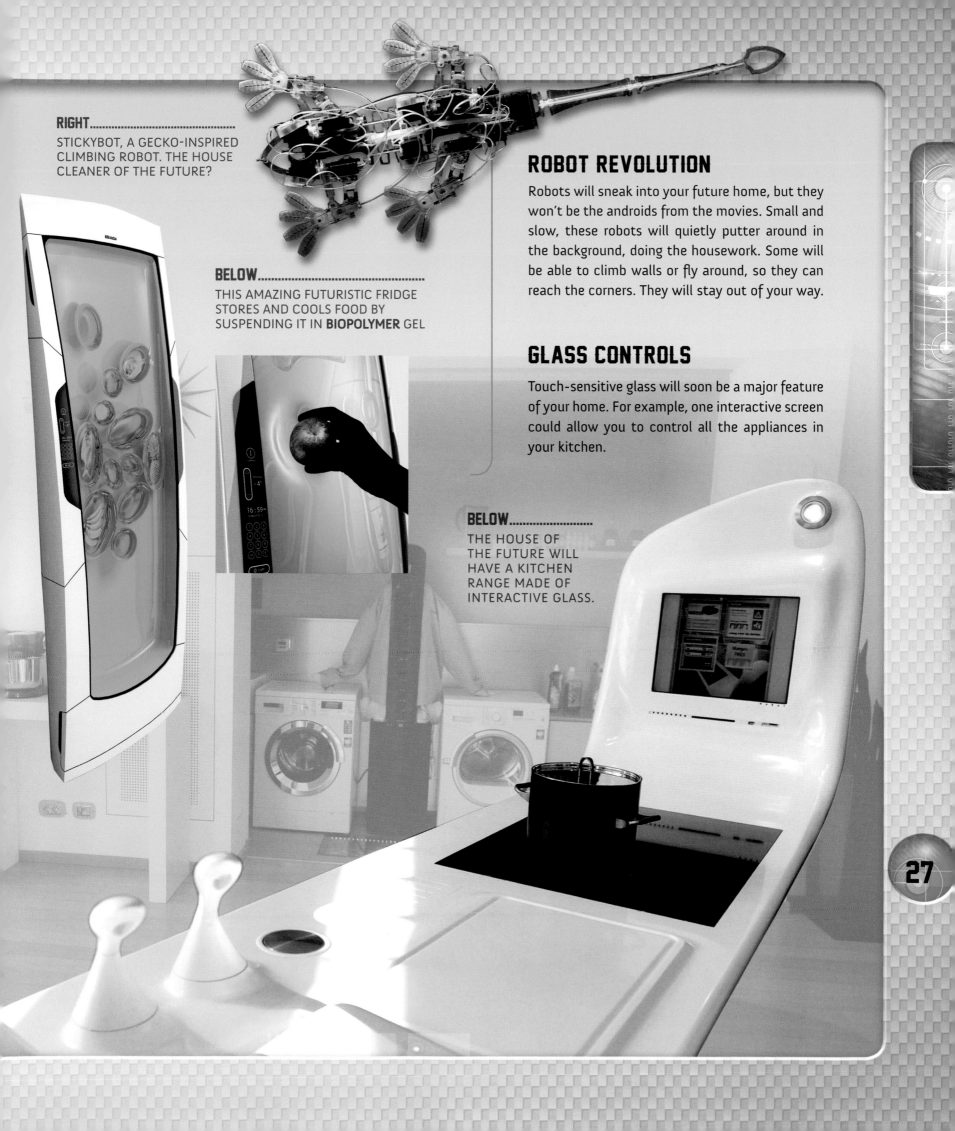

VIRTUAL EDUCATION
THE FUTURE OF LEARNING

The school of the future may not be a place you go to. Online education is taking off, with millions of students already receiving education over the internet, watching lessons/lectures on Web videos, submitting coursework by e-mail, taking part in live chats, and having personal education tailored to their individual needs.

REMOTE LEARNING

Over the next twenty years, a bigger proportion of education will be done via the internet. Students will graduate from top universities without ever having been in the same country as their professors.

DIGITAL TEACHING

The schools that remain might look different. Blackboards will be replaced by interactive glass screens, linked to tablets in every student's hand or as part of their desks. You won't have to go up to the whiteboard to complete an exercise, because what you write on your screen will appear in front of the class. Students will access textbooks with their computer, and upload and download homework this way, too.

BELOW..
NEW TECHNOLOGY MEANS THERE'S
NO MORE NEED FOR PENS OR PAPER.

BELOW..........................
GLASS SCREENS ONLY SHOW WHAT'S ON THE MAIN DISPLAY WITH NO DISTRACTIONS.

CIENCE

HUMAN BODY

LIGHT

EXPERIMENTS

ARTIFICIAL TEACHERS

Teachers might be replaced by robots—a recent experiment in Japan showed that children enjoyed learning English by interacting with a robot programmed to be less able to speak English than they were, so that they learned by teaching the robot teacher.

ABOVE...
THE SAYA TEACHING ROBOT CAN CALL ROLL AND GIVE INSTRUCTIONS LIKE "BE QUIET!"

TOUCH-SENSITIVE GLASS

Touch-sensitive glass could replace blackboards in schools. Imagine if the whole wall was covered with information and graphics that your teacher could move like the buttons on a smartphone!

LEFT...
SIMPLE SHEETS OF GLASS COULD REPLACE MONITORS.

29

WEARABLE TECHNOLOGY
INTELLIGENT CLOTHING

Suppose your jacket could sense the weather and change from keeping you warm to cooling you down? What if your pants turned the heat you create when walking into power to charge your smartphone? Wouldn't it be useful if your swimsuit or skiwear included technology to keep you safe and signal to rescuers in an emergency?

All these scenarios could come true within the next fifteen years thanks to smart fabrics.

ABOVE..........................
THE NIKE FUELBAND
MEASURES HOW
ACTIVE YOU ARE.

WEARABLE ELECTRONICS

Intelligent clothing is made from new or yet-to-be-invented materials that can change the way we think about clothes.

Computers, keyboards, and even screens can be built into fabrics, so you can wear clothes that light up, convert motion and sunlight into electricity, and even double as a computer display. New materials are being developed that are more resistant than ever to heat, cold, radiation, and impacts.

SELF-MENDING FABRIC AND INVISIBILITY CLOAKS

One recently invented fabric not only conducts electricity but can heal itself if cut or torn. Clothes made from this would not only mend themselves, but keep your gadgets connected all the time.

Invisibility cloaks are also being invented. These garments use **fiber optics** to direct light around the body, so that the cloak acts as a screen to project the scene beyond the wearer, masking his or her presence.

LEFT...
THIS SEE-THROUGH COAT FROM THE TACHI LAB IN JAPAN IS MADE OF OPTICAL FIBERS THAT DIRECT LIGHT AROUND THE WEARER.

SURVIVAL SUITS

Perhaps the biggest difference will come in the field of extreme performance clothing such as adventure sportswear, survival clothing, uniforms for emergency workers, and even spacesuits. Researchers have designed the BioSuit: a skintight spacesuit that is less awkward. In the future they plan to include artificial muscles to create a kind of exoskeletal power suit (see page 12).

SMARTWEAR FOR SPORT

If relatively lightweight fabrics can resist the temperature and pressure extremes of space, suits for mountain climbers, deep-sea divers, and extreme snowboarders could become equally light and skintight, while still protecting against even the harshest weather. With built-in radio transmitters, these suits could signal to rescuers in case of an emergency. Skiers could take advantage of airbag-style survival suits in the event of an avalanche. Light and flexible impact-resistant fabrics will become a standard part of extreme sportswear and uniforms of the emergency services.

LEFT.................................
INVENTOR PROFESSOR DAVA NEWMAN SHOWS OFF THE BIOSUIT.

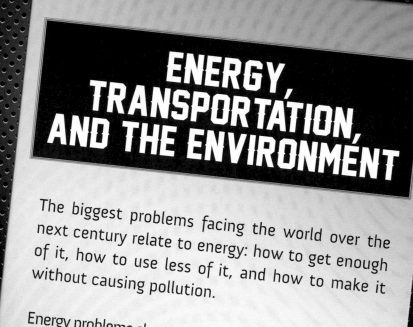

ENERGY, TRANSPORTATION, AND THE ENVIRONMENT

The biggest problems facing the world over the next century relate to energy: how to get enough of it, how to use less of it, and how to make it without causing pollution.

Energy problems shape our approach to transportation, too. How can travel become more energy efficient while also being faster and more comfortable?

This chapter features exciting developments in the science of renewable energy, as well as the faster, greener transportation options of the 21st century.

INSPIRATION FROM THE SUN
NUCLEAR FUSION

The Sun is powered by a process called **nuclear fusion**, which turns minuscule amounts of hot gas into colossal amounts of energy. If we could harness the same process here on Earth, we could generate a lot of cheap energy with virtually no pollution.

$E=MC^2$

Fusion occurs when subatomic particles get squashed together so hard and at such high temperatures that they fuse or merge. The resulting particle is slightly lighter (i.e., less massive) than the original ones, and as is expressed by Einstein's famous equation $E=mc^2$, a little bit of mass equals an enormous amount of energy.

THE BREAKEVEN CHALLENGE

Fusion power uses a form of hydrogen that is found in seawater, and produces no waste gases and virtually no radioactive waste. If it can be made to work, this process could convert small amounts of cheap fuel into a huge supply of energy.

Unfortunately the technology of nuclear fusion is very hard to get right. The fuel must be heated and squashed, and this requires a lot of energy. After 60 years of research, scientists are still at least 20 years away from making usable fusion.

RIGHT...
THE INTERIOR OF GERMANY'S ASDEX
(AXIALLY SYMMETRIC DIVERTOR EXPERIMENT)
UPGRADE FUSION REACTOR.

LASERS AND TOKAMAKS

At the National Ignition Facility in California, 192 high-powered lasers are focused on a tiny pellet of fuel, causing it to explode into a ball of hot gas called plasma. The shock waves from the explosion smash the plasma into a tiny point, and this is then heated with another laser blast so that it ignites—i.e., the fusion reaction begins.

Meanwhile, in Europe, a project called ITER is currently planning to build a fusion reactor in France. Here, plasma is heated up by blasting it with microwaves and beams of particles traveling at close to the speed of light. Then it is crushed by massive magnetic fields until fusion is achieved. This kind of reactor is called a **tokamak**.

However, the cost of ITER has now reached more than 20.4 billion dollars and the completion date has been delayed until 2020. The actual firing-up of the reactor is not going to happen until 2027.

ABOVE...
TOKAMAK FUSION TEST REACTOR
AT PRINCETON UNIVERSITY, NJ.

FUTURE ENERGY
GREEN POWER

Most of our energy comes from burning **fossil fuels**. This is getting more expensive because it is running out and/or becoming harder to get out of the ground. Nuclear power is one possible replacement, but nuclear fission can be dangerous and dirty.

However, there are several energy sources that are freely available, clean, and will never run out: sunlight, wind, waves, and heat from the ground (geothermal).

WIND ENERGY

Wind energy is already harvested with turbines (below), but many people dislike them, and they only harvest wind near ground level. The wind is much stronger higher up in the atmosphere, so exciting new technology using kites and balloons is now under development

BELOW..
WIND FARMS LIKE THIS ARE BECOMING
A FAMILIAR SIGHT WORLDWIDE.

ABOVE..
AN ARTIST'S IMPRESSION OF "SEA SNAKE"
WAVE POWER MACHINES MADE BY PELAMIS.

OCEAN POWER

Another form of energy is wave power (waves are mostly caused by the wind blowing across the sea), and the sea also provides power as the tide ebbs and flows.

One design for a wave power generator is the "sea snake"—a long tube or chain of linked tubes riding on the waves. These tubes rise and fall as waves move along them. Power is generated either from the bending of joints or the squashing and stretching of the tube. Another design, called the Oyster, uses a giant metal clamshell pump; passing waves push the clamshell closed, working the pump, which drives water to an onshore power generator similar to a water mill.

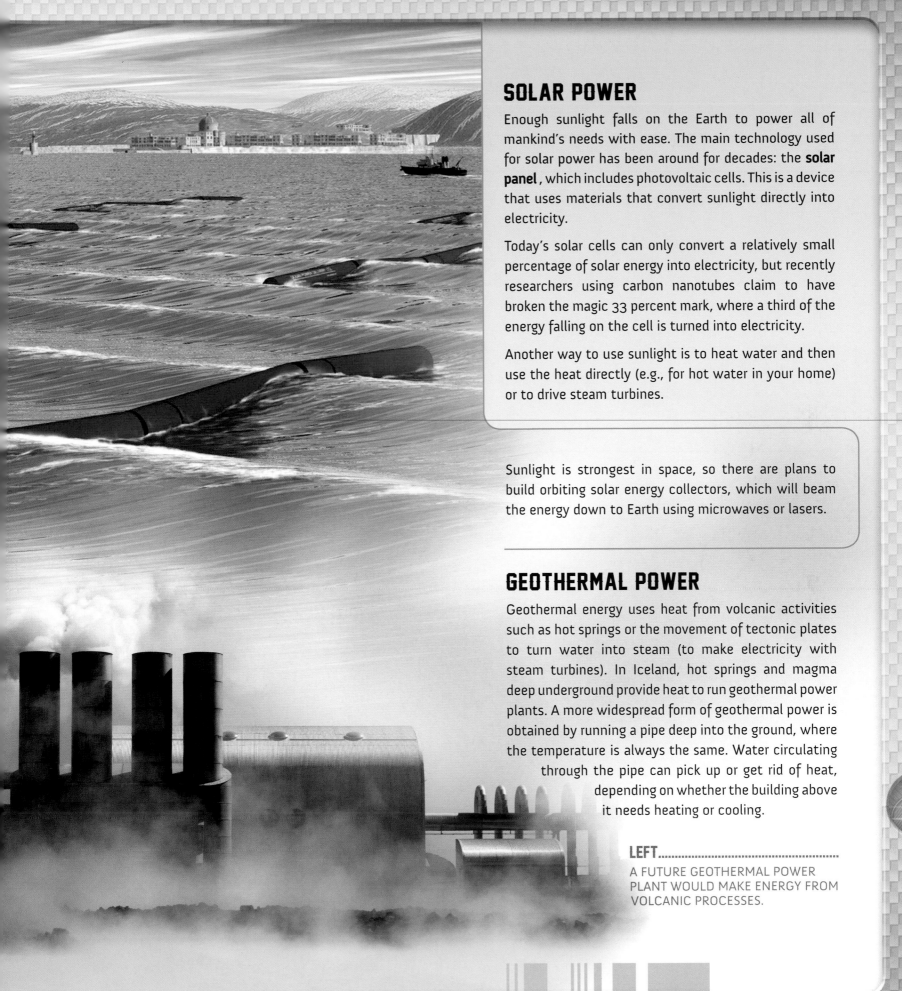

SOLAR POWER

Enough sunlight falls on the Earth to power all of mankind's needs with ease. The main technology used for solar power has been around for decades: the **solar panel**, which includes photovoltaic cells. This is a device that uses materials that convert sunlight directly into electricity.

Today's solar cells can only convert a relatively small percentage of solar energy into electricity, but recently researchers using carbon nanotubes claim to have broken the magic 33 percent mark, where a third of the energy falling on the cell is turned into electricity.

Another way to use sunlight is to heat water and then use the heat directly (e.g., for hot water in your home) or to drive steam turbines.

Sunlight is strongest in space, so there are plans to build orbiting solar energy collectors, which will beam the energy down to Earth using microwaves or lasers.

GEOTHERMAL POWER

Geothermal energy uses heat from volcanic activities such as hot springs or the movement of tectonic plates to turn water into steam (to make electricity with steam turbines). In Iceland, hot springs and magma deep underground provide heat to run geothermal power plants. A more widespread form of geothermal power is obtained by running a pipe deep into the ground, where the temperature is always the same. Water circulating through the pipe can pick up or get rid of heat, depending on whether the building above it needs heating or cooling.

LEFT.................................
A FUTURE GEOTHERMAL POWER PLANT WOULD MAKE ENERGY FROM VOLCANIC PROCESSES.

GREEN POWER
SOLAR LOOP

The Solar Loop, an outdoor event space, consists of two different surfaces that twist into one another. The photovoltaic surface is always exposed to the Sun, while the mirrored surface reflects light from the surrounding area. The shape of the structure allows it to follow the arc of the Sun at its best angle over the course of the day.

If the project goes ahead, the loop could be built on a small scale—the size of a pavilion—or on a huge scale, depending on budget.

ABOVE
THE SOLAR LOOP COULD BE USED FOR CONCERTS AND OTHER PUBLIC EVENTS.

BELOW
ARTIST'S DRAWING OF THE SOLAR LOOP IN THE SUNSHINE.

CLEANING UP
EASING CLIMATE CHANGE

Thanks to the billions of tons of carbon dioxide (CO_2) and other **greenhouse gases** pumped into the atmosphere by humans, the world is warming up. This is causing ice caps to melt, sea levels to rise, and weather to change, including more and bigger storms and changes to seasonal weather patterns.

What can we do to combat this?

DIRECT ACTION

Worries about **global warming** have led to efforts to reduce the amount of greenhouse gas we produce, but these efforts have been slow to materialize. New technologies and successful 'green' business ventures may encourage innovation and government policy to help lead the way.

CARBON SCRUBBING AND FREEZING

One idea is to remove CO_2 from the air with large-scale **carbon scrubbers**. These use chemical "sponges" to soak up carbon from the air. They are common in submarines and spaceships. To help with reducing greenhouse gases on an industrial scale, they would need to be as big as factories and use renewable energy.

Technology on that scale will take a while, but in the meantime some high-tech companies are developing air capture systems that will take CO_2 from the air and recycle it to manufacture ultra-low emission fuels.

40

SOLUTIONS

SIMPLE AND ECO-FRIENDLY WAYS TO COUNTERACT GLOBAL WARMING MIGHT INCLUDE:

→ reforestation (planting trees);

→ painting our roofs white to prevent the absorption of heat;

→ dumping iron filings into the ocean to fertilize algae, which soaks up CO_2 (but unfortunately also poisons marine life).

A MAGNIFIED PICTURE OF PLANKTONIC ALGAE THAT HAVE BEEN
FERTILIZED BY IRON FILINGS. ALGAE HELP TO SOAK UP CO2.

MORE IMPRESSIVE, SCIENCE-FICTION STYLE, PLANS INCLUDE:

→ giant mirrors in space to stop sunlight from reaching
Earth;

→ colossal guns to fire millions of ceramic discs
into low orbit for the same reason;

→ a system of massive refrigerators in Antarctica
where temperatures are already low and there is
plenty of wind to supply power. These would
freeze billions of tons of CO2 out of the air
before storing it somehow.

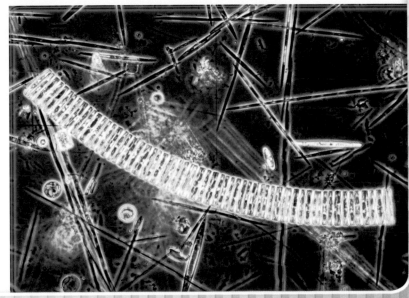

41

POWER PACKED
ELECTRICITY MOVES ON

What if the battery in your cell phone could last for months on a single charge, or a box the size of a microwave oven could power your home? This is the promise of **fuel cell** technology.

A fuel cell converts chemical energy into electricity. So does a battery, but a fuel cell can be refueled, whereas a battery has to be replaced or recharged. Fuel cells are also good because the only waste they produce is water.

HOW HYDROGEN FUEL CELLS WORK

If you burn hydrogen in oxygen you get dihydrogen monoxide, aka water. If you do this reaction in a fuel cell, it is possible to siphon off **electrons** from the hydrogen and pass them through a circuit to light a bulb or drive a motor. Fuel cells use pure hydrogen, which is difficult to store because it must be kept super-cold and tends to explode if there is a leak. Or they use other fuels like alcohol, which are converted into hydrogen.

FUEL CELLS TODAY

Fuel cells have several advantages. They convert energy from the chemicals into useful power. They supply a constant feed of electricity. They come in different sizes, from huge power plants for factories, to smaller fuel cells for cars, and tiny cartridges for laptops and cell phones.

Today fuel cells are used by companies like Google; by the military; and by travelers who need long-lasting portable power sources.

HYDROSTIK® PRO

LWH22-10L-5(PRO)

⚠ WARNING
• Contents are flammable. Do not disassemble.
• Avoid contact with contents.

ABOVE

THE HYDROSTIK IS A HYDROGEN CARTRIDGE AVAILABLE TO BUY IN STORES.

FUTURE POWER

Fuel cells have a lot of problems. They are very expensive to build and need fuel, which has to come from somewhere. Hydrogen is hard to make and mostly comes from fossil fuels at the moment.

Researchers are working on these problems. It is hoped that by 2025 fuel cells will be much cheaper, while hydrogen fuels could be widely produced using green power plants.

ABOVE...
THE FUEL CELL "ENGINE" OF A VAUXHALL ZAFIRA.

ABOVE.................................
ELECTRIC CARS, LIKE THIS BMW13, ARE ON THE ROAD NOW. CARS WITH FUEL CELL ENGINES ARE IN DEVELOPMENT.

ARTIFICIAL PHOTOSYNTHESIS

Plants have a system of their own for converting one form of energy into another, **photosynthesis**.

Researchers are trying to copy this process and even improve on it. If they make a breakthrough, artificial plants could harvest sunlight to make both fuel and electricity.

LEFT...
COULD ARTIFICIAL PLANTS HARVEST SUNLIGHT TO CREATE ELECTRICITY?

THE FUTURE OF FLIGHT
PASSENGER AIRPLANES AND AIRSHIPS

Air travel faces a number of problems over the next two decades. Airplanes burn huge quantities of expensive fuel, creating pollution. Meanwhile, many passengers want to get where they are going faster. The aerospace industry has come up with some exciting answers to these challenges.

SWARMS AND SLINGSHOTS

Leading the pack is the aircraft manufacturer Airbus, which recently advanced some ambitious concepts.

To save fuel and make their airplanes more efficient, they have proposed that airplanes fly in swarms (i.e., close together), so that following airplanes experience less drag. This would require close control by advanced computer systems.

Airplanes use much of their fuel during takeoff, so Airbus has suggested that a massive slingshot could be used to accelerate planes on the runway, catapulting them into the air at high speeds.

ABOVE ....
AIRBUS'S CONCEPT FOR THE CABIN OF THE FUTURE.

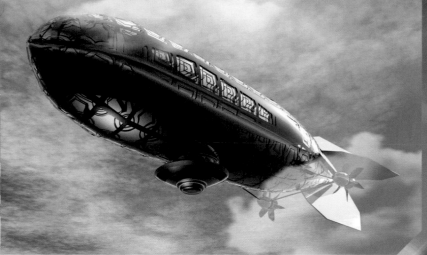

AIRSHIPS OF THE FUTURE

Before airplanes, there were airships, also known as blimps, dirigibles, or Zeppelins. The technology is still in use today. They are lifted by lighter-than-air bags of gas so that the aircraft does not need to spend energy getting into the air and staying there. Airships have had to overcome many technical problems. Originally they used dangerously flammable hydrogen gas. Even today they have problems with ballast (heavy weights used to make the airship go up and down).

New airship designs claim to have overcome these problems. The U.S. military has tried to develop airships for cargo lifting and surveillance. One solution is the Hybrid Air Vehicle (HAV)—an airship where the balloon part is shaped like a large, fat wing, so it generates its own lift, as well as harnessing lift from the helium inside it. According to its makers, the HAV combines the best features of airships and airplanes, and is easier to control than a normal airship.

FLYING WINGS

Other manufacturers have suggested new wing and body designs, such as wide, flat bodies that act like wings, generating their own lift (and known as flying wings or lifting bodies), or wraparound wings to improve aerodynamics. NASA and Boeing have collaborated on the X-48 prototype, which uses the flying-wing shape to cut fuel use. However, airplanes like this would have no passenger windows.

In contrast, Airbus has suggested that new materials might make it possible to have aircraft with transparent walls, so passengers can have 360° views. Another development to improve passenger comfort could be morphing seats, which would mold themselves to the individual.

HIGH-FLYING VULTURE

Airship designs that are either in planning or already flying include the Long Endurance Multi-Intelligence Vehicle, which had a test flight in 2012. The Vulture program involves a lightweight but gigantic wing, which stays permanently at high altitude as a cheap alternative to a satellite. It may use airship technology as well as self-powering solar cells.

Airships could also be used to haul cargo, and to help traffic control and disaster-response teams with surveillance.

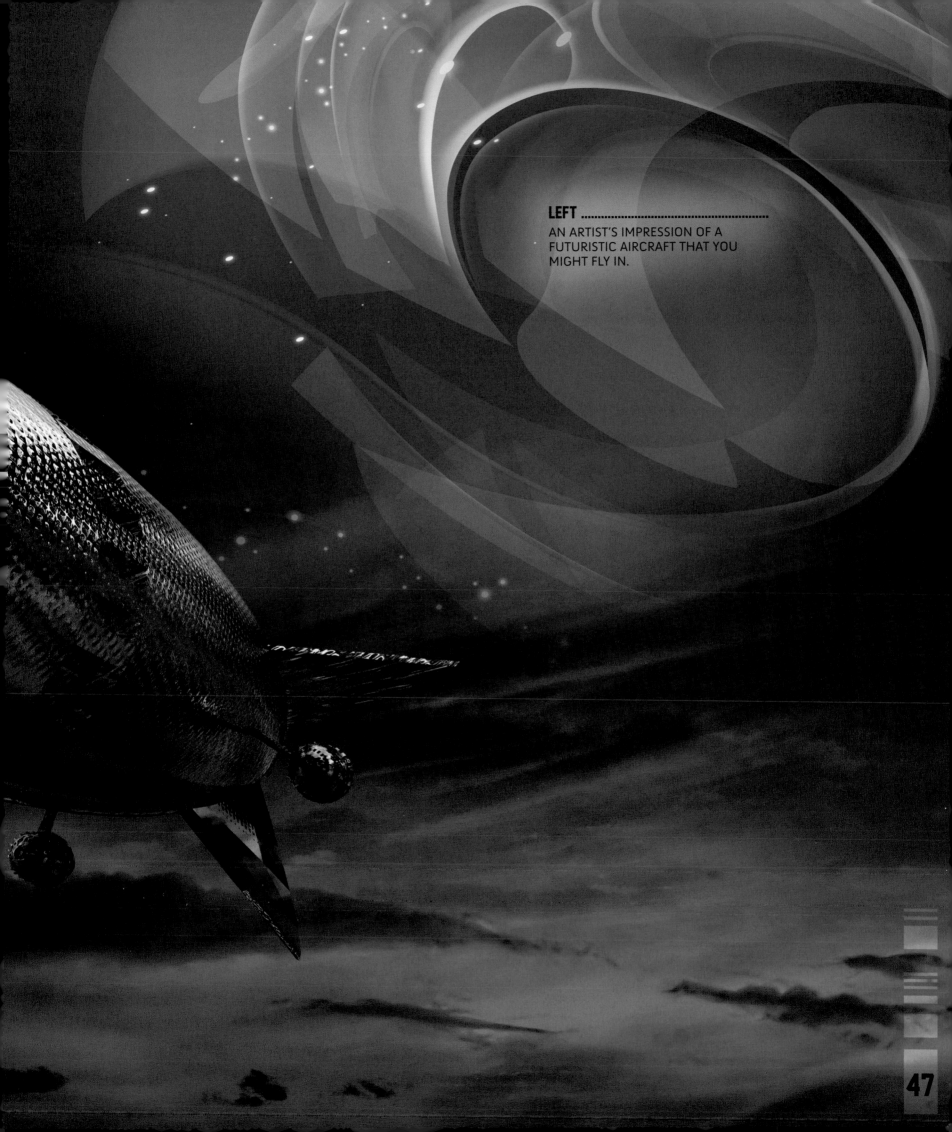

LEFT ....
AN ARTIST'S IMPRESSION OF A
FUTURISTIC AIRCRAFT THAT YOU
MIGHT FLY IN.

FLYING CARS

Inventors have been dreaming of flying cars since before the first airplane, but it wasn't until the 1960s that the idea became popular. There was great optimism that new technology could revolutionize daily life, and a flying car was one of the ways of achieving this. In 2012, you could buy a vehicle that you could both drive and fly.

BELOW.....
THE AMAZING HAMMERHEAD FLIES USING THREE FANS THAT TILT AND THRUST.

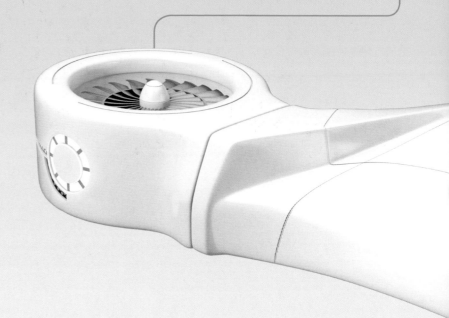

ROADABLE AIRCRAFT

The most successful early efforts to build a flying car were Robert Fulton's 1946 Airphibian and the related Aerocar designed and built by Moulton Taylor in the 1960s.

Driver-pilots still had the problem of finding a runway for takeoff and landing. These vehicles were more like an airplane than a car. In fact this type of vehicle is known as a "**roadable aircraft**." The latest and most advanced roadable aircraft is the Terrafugia Transition (right), which has folding wings and four wheels, but still needs a runway.

BELOW.....
THE TERRAFUGIA TRANSITION, A FLYING CAR THAT YOU CAN BUY TODAY ($279,000!)

48

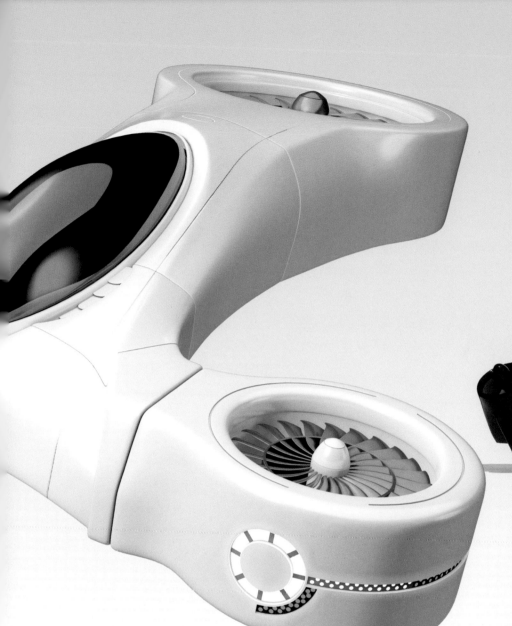

SKYCARS AND FAN CRAFT

A "real" flying car is one that can take off vertically from the middle of a line of traffic, fly across town, and touch down outside your garage. The nearest thing to this today is the Moller Skycar, which combines the looks of a Ferrari with the power of four fan blades, also known as ducted propellers or shrouded rotors. These are like small helicopter rotors inside hoops or ducts. They are enclosed, safe to use, produce lots of power, and can be angled for vertical takeoff and landing.

ABOVE..
THE MOLLER SKYCAR AUTOMATES FLIGHT CONTROLS, AND IS DESIGNED FOR ANYONE WHO CAN DRIVE.

BELOW..
AUTOMATED SKYWAYS WILL MAKE IT SAFE FOR HUGE NUMBERS OF VEHICLES TO FLY AT ONCE.

SKYWAYS

Flying cars could cause real problems—millions of small aircraft could lead to horrible accidents in the skies. Advances in computer control and navigation should create "skyways"—highways in the sky. NASA is coordinating a "highway in the sky" project that aims to integrate GPS and automated-sensor technology with augmented-reality screens to generate computer-drawn skyways for driver-pilots to follow, while computers prevent collisions.

49

MAG-LEV

The world's fastest trains use magnetic levitation, or **mag-lev,** to overcome drag and friction. They travel super-fast.

Electromagnets are used to generate strong magnetic forces that allow the train to hover above the rails (i.e., levitate). Since the train and the rail do not touch, there is no friction, and mag-lev trains can reach speeds of up to 268 mph (431 kph).

LEFT..
WILL ELECTROMAGNETIC MONORAILS BE THE TRANSPORTATION OF THE FUTURE?

A NEW AGE OF SAIL

KITESHIPS AND FLOATING CITIES

Hundreds of years ago, ships used wind power to get around. Now ships have engines, but the advantages that wind offers are still the same today as in the great age of sailing ships. The wind is free to use, weighs nothing, causes no pollution, and never runs out.

The same cannot be said for bunker fuel, the type of oil that most ships run on. Bunker fuel is the dirtiest and most polluting form of vehicle fuel, and carbon dioxide emissions from shipping are growing all the time.

SKYSAILS

To solve these problems, some shipping companies are exploring the idea of using new spins on sailing technology to harness the power of the wind, cut their fuel costs, and reduce pollution.

One idea is the **kiteship**, a normal cargo vessel fitted with a giant kite or skysail that can be automatically winched back in and folded away when the wind is not blowing. By flying the skysail at a high altitude, the ship takes advantage of high wind speeds.

VERTICAL WINGS

Another idea is to replace the fabric sails of a sailing ship with metal wings, similar to those on an airplane but vertical.

Researchers at the University of Tokyo have designed the Wind Challenger Project, a system of retractable metal wings or aerofoils. Just as an airplane's wings generate lift, the aerofoil sails generate a force pushing the wings and the attached boat. The computer-controlled sails can rotate. In stormy weather they can telescope down into the hull.

LEFT...
THE STATE-OF-THE-ART B9 SAILSHIP COULD BE CREATED USING EXISTING TECHNOLOGY.

BELOW...
LILYPAD ECOPOLIS IS A VISION OF A FUTURE HOME
FOR "CLIMATE REFUGEES" DISPLACED BY THE EFFECTS
OF GLOBAL WARMING OVER THE NEXT CENTURY.

FLOATING CITIES AND SEAGOING SKYSCRAPERS

New sailing ships are not the only bold idea planned for
the oceans. A variety of exciting new projects imagine
whole communities at sea—on artificial islands, floating
cities, or giant ocean-going marine observatories. The
Sea Orbiter project, supposedly set to launch in 2014,
is a skyscraper-like ocean laboratory, observatory, and
exploration vessel that will extend over 98 feet (30 m)
down below the surface of the water as well as over
65 feet (20 m) above it.

RIGHT...
THE SEA ORBITER IS LIKE A POINTED ICEBERG,
WITH MOST OF ITS MASS BELOW THE SURFACE.

BEAM ME UP
LASER-POWERED LIGHTCRAFT

Revolutionary technology straight out of science fiction allows saucer-shaped spaceships, known as **lightcraft**, to be accelerated to hypersonic speeds by blasting them with lasers fired from space. It would be possible to travel anywhere in the world within 45 minutes, or out into space at a fraction of the cost of launching today's rockets.

With orbiting power plants, rotating spacecraft, superconducting electromagnetic propulsion, and ion thrusters, this incredible scheme pushes the boundaries of scientific imagination but is entirely based on existing technology.

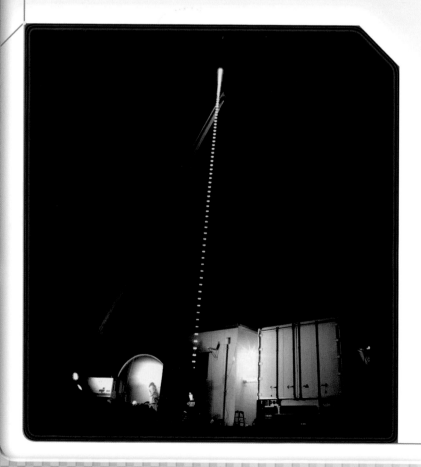

LEFT...............................
RESEARCHERS TESTING A "SPINNING TOP."

RIGHT...............................
A METAL "SPINNING TOP" USED IN TESTING THE PHYSICS OF LIGHTCRAFT.

LEFT..
THE MICROWAVE LIGHTCRAFT CONCEPT FROM NASA.

BEAM PROPULSION

The bottom or sides of a lightcraft are dish-shaped mirrors. When a laser or similarly intense beam of energy hits the mirror, it is focused onto a point directly behind the craft, heating the air to a temperature hotter than the surface of the Sun. The intense heat instantly vaporizes the air, creating an explosive shock wave that blasts the lightcraft forward. Every pulse of laser light that hits the craft creates another explosion. The string of explosions accelerates it to great speed. This is called beam propulsion.

There are at least two plans for full-size lightcraft. One plan, developed by beam-propulsion pioneer Dr. Leik Myrabo and the Umea Institute, calls for a scaled-up version of the spinning-top design.

FLYING SAUCERS

An even more ambitious design, codeveloped by Myrabo with NASA, uses **masers**—microwave lasers—fired from an orbiting satellite. The satellite collects sunlight to power the microwave beam and fires it down onto a saucer-shaped lightcraft, which has collecting mirrors that route the power to one side of the craft, causing a string of explosions that accelerate it sideways. Once it is going fast enough, the lightcraft turns so it is lying flat, face toward the airstream.

The lightcraft now focuses the maser beam ahead of it to create an airspike—a bubble of superheated air that explodes in front of the lightcraft. Immediately behind the airspike's explosive shock wave there is no air, just a vacuum, which means the lightcraft experiences no air resistance or drag. It can accelerate to about 18,645 mph (30,000 kph) using electromagnetically powered **ion drives** around its edge.

LEFT..
CONCEPT FOR A LIGHTSHIP AND LAUNCH PLATFORM FROM AURORA SPACELINES.

ROBOT EXPLORERS
DRONES

"Drone" is a general term for a remote-controlled vehicle or robot. Today, it usually means an **unmanned air vehicle** (UAV), a radio-controlled small aircraft such as the Predator drones used by the U.S. military. Drones come in all shapes and sizes, and can be found on land and sea and in the air.

The robot submarines known as ROVs (remotely operated vehicles—see page 77) are a type of drone, as are bomb disposal robots used by the police and military. A drone is a sort of telepresence robot (see page 8).

THE CHEAP ALTERNATIVE

Drones are used by the military, but in the next 15 years they are likely to become common everywhere.

People are valuable and getting them somewhere is expensive. Why send a reporter and camera crew to a remote, war-torn district when you can send a drone for a fraction of the cost?

ABOVE AND BELOW
THE RQ-4A GLOBAL HAWK IS A RECONNAISSANCE DRONE USED BY THE U.S. AND CANADIAN MILITARY.

KEEPING AN EYE OUT

Most of the drones in use today are expensive radio-controlled aircraft, such as the quadcopter drones (lightweight flying robots with four mini-rotors) used for newsgathering in Nebraska, but there is a huge range of experimental drones already at prototype stage.

The Electric Power Research Institute is developing small drones to fly out after a storm and locate downed power lines, while the U.S. Coast Guard is considering unmanned boat drones.

LEFT..
SATOORN IS A FRENCH-DESIGNED UAV THAT CAN BE USED INSIDE BUILDINGS.

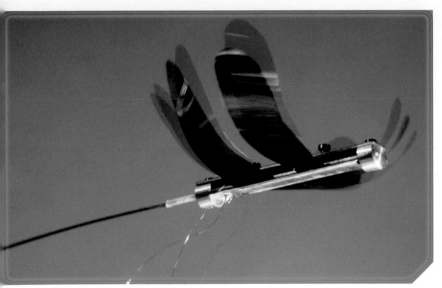

MICRO-UAVS

Already taking flight in the laboratory are tiny, remote-controlled aircraft. Quadcopters are widely available as toys, and programs have been developed to make them fly as swarms. Dragonflies, bees, and birds have inspired biomimetic micro-UAVs. The SilMach dragonfly drone uses flapping wings to propel itself.

Bounce Imaging has developed the Smart Ball, a small sphere packed with sensors that can be tossed into damaged buildings or dropped down dangerous holes to send back information to rescuers.

ABOVE................................
SILMACH'S DRAGONFLY SURVEILLANCE MICRODRONE IS ONLY 2.5 INCHES (6.5 CM) WIDE.

LEFT......................................
THE NANO HUMMINGBIRD FROM AEROVIRONMENT IS ONLY SLIGHTLY LARGER THAN A REAL BIRD.

CLEANING THE OCEANS

Drones don't have to look at things. Suggestions for useful drone activities include cleaning robots, which can be scattered into the sea to clean up oil spills, and plastic-eating drone submarines that could wander the ocean picking up the plastic garbage that has been dumped by humans.

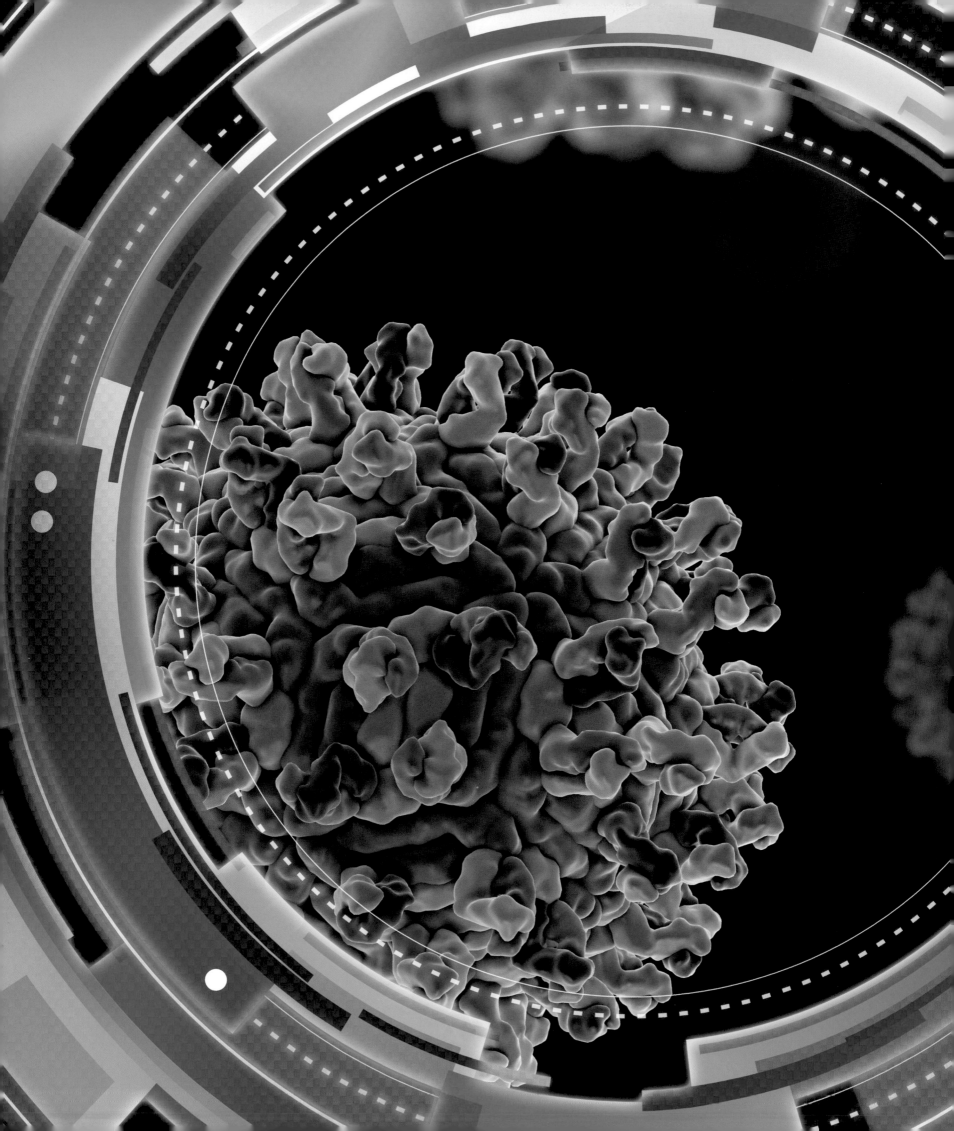

MEDICINE AND BIOTECHNOLOGY

Medicine is still waiting for the super-apps of the genetic engineering revolution, but they could be on their way. They will have a huge impact on all aspects of life, not just health and medicine.

Treatments and even cures for deadly diseases could be on the way thanks to genetic biotechnology. Robotics big and small will make an impact on health, from tiny nanobots that patrol your blood vessels to bionic arms and legs for the disabled.

Biotechnology may make it possible to bring extinct species back to life.

HEART-HEALING MINI-MACHINES
MEDICAL NANOBOTS

In the 1966 science-fiction movie *Fantastic Voyage*, a submarine is shrunk to microscopic size and injected into the bloodstream of an injured man, on a mission to save his life. The microchip swims through his blood vessels and performs laser surgery from inside.

Today, the world's leading research institutes are working on making this science fiction into fact by creating nanomachines a little bigger than atoms, which might be able to patrol our bodies in the future.

SMALLEST OF THE SMALL

Nanomachines are built from individual molecules or even just a few atoms. "Nano" means "tiny", and nanomachines are machines built on the nanometer scale. To give you an idea of how small that is, find a metric rule and look at the millimeter mark. Now imagine splitting that into a million smaller pieces. Each one of those pieces is a nanometer. A human hair is around 90,000 nanometers across.

A NANO REVOLUTION

During the industrial revolution, big machines took over many complicated tasks.

This time, **nanobots** are taking on jobs too small for the human hand. They work with individual atoms and molecules, moving things, picking them up and even destroying them. They could make it possible to inject tiny robots into the bloodstream to attack germs, clear blocked arteries, and fix broken nerve or muscle cells.

ABOVE...
AN ARTIST'S DRAWING OF A MEDICAL NANOBOT AT WORK ON A BLOOD CELL.

BUBBLE-POWERED NANOROCKETS

Scientists have already created bubble-powered rocket nanobots in the laboratory. A layer of material a few atoms thick is rolled into a tube and filled with hydrogen peroxide, which reacts with water to make bubbles. When placed into water, the tiny rocket shoots a stream of bubbles out of one end, driving it forward.

Nanoparticles have been developed to carry luminous blobs of chemical on one end. The other end of the nanoparticle is fitted with a molecule that sticks onto diseased cells. When a dose of these nanoparticles is injected into the body, they find their target and light up, so doctors can locate the problem.

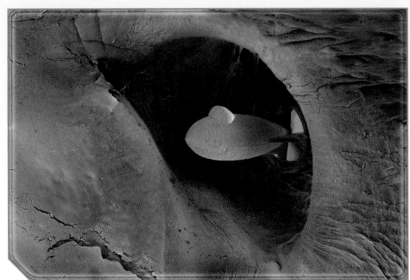

ABOVE..
A NANOSUBMARINE, CREATED BY MICROTEC, TRAVELS THROUGH AN ARTERY.

FUTURE NANOBOTS

In the future, nanobots could be built that can live inside the body for long periods, finding their own way around and locating trouble spots. Some could be equipped as hunter-killers to track down viruses, bacteria, and cancerous cells. Others could be fitted with cutting equipment to clear clogged arteries.

BIONIC PEOPLE
PROSTHETICS AND ENHANCEMENTS

The stars of the 2012 Paralympic Games were the blade runners—lower-leg amputees whose missing limbs were replaced with springy, blade-like prosthetics (an artificial body part). These high-tech blades, made from advanced materials, are so good at storing and releasing energy that they have caused a big argument over whether they boost human performance.

Exciting new technology is transforming the world of prosthetics. Recent advances mean that prosthetic feet, hands, and other parts that function as well as the real thing will soon be available. By 2025, artificial limbs could be better than the real thing.

RIGHT............................
PROSTHETIC LEGS
NOW USE SPRINGS TO
MIMIC NATURAL MOTION.

TYPES OF PROSTHESES

Prosthetic legs come in three categories:

➜   ordinary prostheses, which are basically similar to wooden legs.

➜   energy-storing-and-returning (ESR) feet, which use springs and small motors to mimic the action of natural feet, ankles, and legs.

➜   **bionic** legs, which are connected to the user's nervous system, making it possible to control them directly.

FEET 2.0

The Belgian Ankle Mimicking Prosthetic Foot (AMP foot) prosthesis is a recent breakthrough in ESR technology. Many ESR feet have springs that act as the tendons of the foot. The AMP foot includes a lightweight motor that mimics natural muscles.

The Rehabilitation Institute of Chicago recently developed a bionic leg that can respond to the user's nervous system. A company called Bebionic has developed a bionic hand that responds to signals from nerves in the user's upper arm, making it possible to open bottles, make a fist, and even type. The fingers are controlled by thought alone.

ABOVE..
BRITISH ATHLETE JONNIE PEACOCK WINS THE
100 M SPRINT AT THE 2012 PARALYMPICS.

TENTACLE ARMS AND FINGER TOOLS

By 2025 bionic hands and feet could give the disabled extra abilities, and maybe even extra strength and endurance, with infinitely rotating wrists and bendable fingers, and extra fingers with changeable tools.

ABOVE..
THE BEBIONIC ARTIFICIAL HAND HAS
FOURTEEN DIFFERENT GRIP MOTIONS.

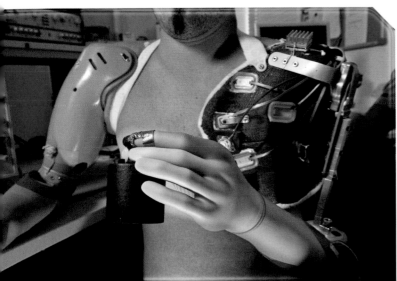

INVISIBLE MUSCLE SUITS

Bionics might advance to the point where a completely paralyzed person could control a wearable exoskeleton. A "muscle suit" could be worn hidden under clothes.

LEFT..
A MIND-CONTROLLED ROBOTIC ARM,
PIONEERED BY OTTO BOCK HEALTHCARE.

HACKING NATURE
BIOENGINEERING AND CLONING

Bioengineering means changing the way nature works through the use of technology. One example is the growth of animal cells in the laboratory.

This leads to a whole range of possibilities. What if we could solve the global food crisis by growing meat in a test tube? What if we could cure illness by spraying a cloud of special benign viruses down our throats? And what if we could bring extinct creatures back to life, so that you could see a real live mammoth at the zoo?

BELOW..................................
AN ARTIST'S IMPRESSION OF A HERD OF MAMMOTHS. COULD WE SOON SEE THIS FOR REAL?

THE VACANTI MOUSE

In a famous experiment in 1997, a U.S. scientist implanted a laboratory-grown ear (made from cow cells) into the back of a mouse, proving that it is possible to grow replacement body parts.

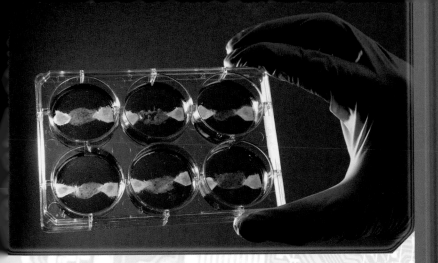

TEST-TUBE MEAT

Recently, research has enabled the growth of replacement parts for human kidneys. In the future it might be possible to grow new parts for the eye, the heart, the spinal cord, the liver, the bones, and muscles.

Human cells are not the only ones that can be bioengineered. Scientists are working on ways to grow animal muscle cells in the lab. If they succeed, you could be eating a beefburger made from meat that doesn't come from an actual cow.

ABOVE..
ANIMAL CELLS BEING GROWN IN A PETRI DISH.

THE REAL JURASSIC PARK

Cloning is growing an identical copy of an animal by implanting its DNA into an egg, which then develops into an adult animal. In the film *Jurassic Park*, scientists use dinosaur DNA to clone dinosaurs, but the dinosaurs died out 65 million years ago and DNA cannot survive that long.

However, DNA has been recovered from the bodies of frozen mammoths. It could be possible to clone these and other extinct animals. DNA could be taken from a mammoth's corpse and inserted into the egg of an elephant, which would grow into a baby mammoth carried by a female elephant.

Other extinct animals that could be brought back from the dead include the saber-toothed cat, the dodo, the giant sloth, the moa, and the thylacine wolf.

ABOVE..
SCIENTISTS COULD RECOVER DNA FROM
FROZEN MAMMOTHS LIKE THIS ONE.

GENETIC ENGINEERING

Genetic engineering occurs when scientists tinker with the genetic makeup of a living organism. Every organism has a genetic code made from **DNA**, which is carried inside every cell. This blueprint contains the instructions for making and running the organism, and these instructions can be changed.

Gene therapies are also under development for conditions from hemophilia to Parkinson's disease, so it may soon be routine to treat disease by spraying an engineered virus down your throat so that it can get into your bloodstream.

RIGHT............................
MODEL DNA STRANDS.

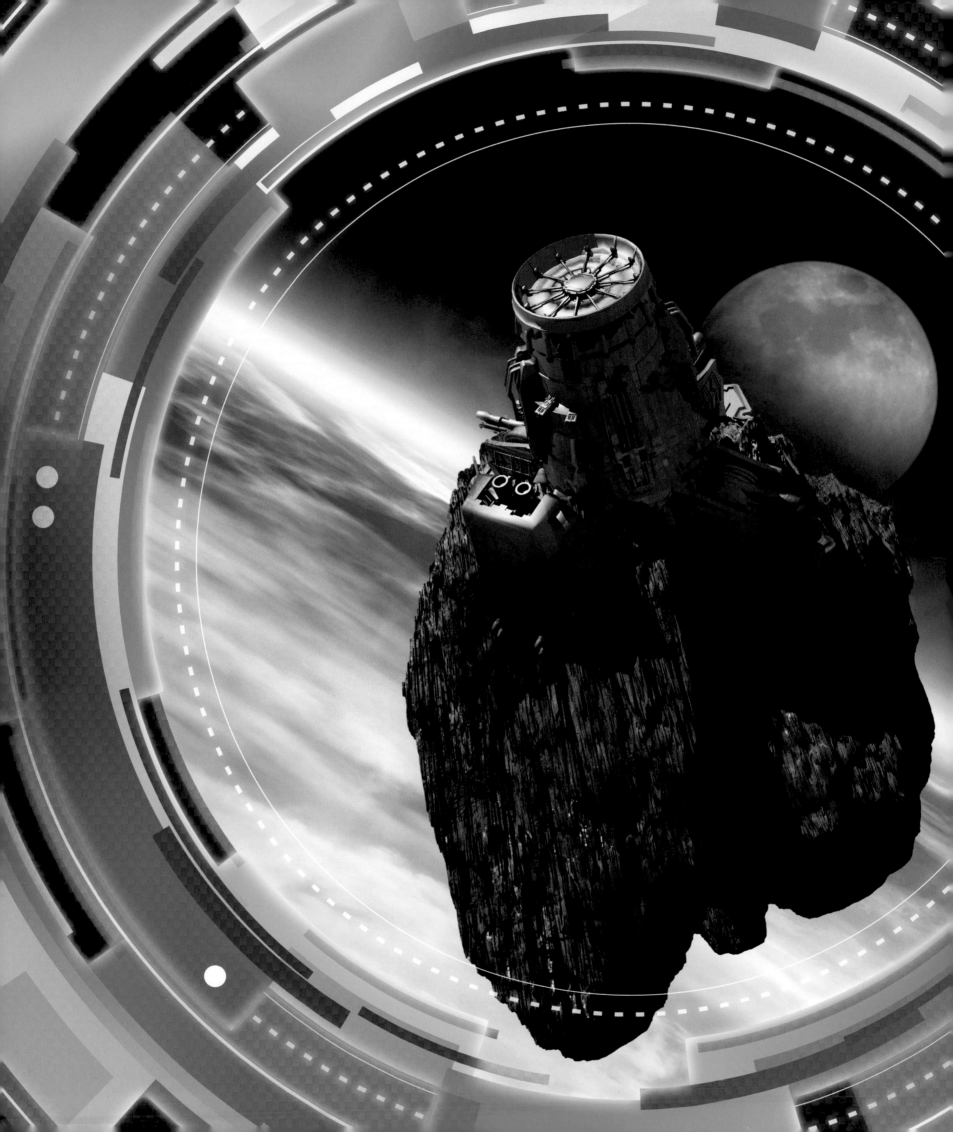

EXPLORATION

Exciting developments in space travel mean that within twenty years many people will be able to afford a trip into space. Private space travel is driving the space industry forward at its fastest rate in decades. Private spacecraft already deliver supplies to the International Space Station.

Advanced technology is being aimed down as well as up. High-tech submarines explore the extremes of the ocean and undersea mining colonies harvest the riches of the deep.

TICKET TO THE MOON
PRIVATE SPACE FLIGHT

Rockets developed, built, and flown by governments tend to be expensive. The biggest rocket available to the U.S. government, the Delta 4, costs around $435 million per launch.

Space shuttle launches were similarly expensive. When the space shuttle fleet was coming to the end of its lifespan, the U.S. government decided to use private companies to send supplies to the International Space Station (ISS).

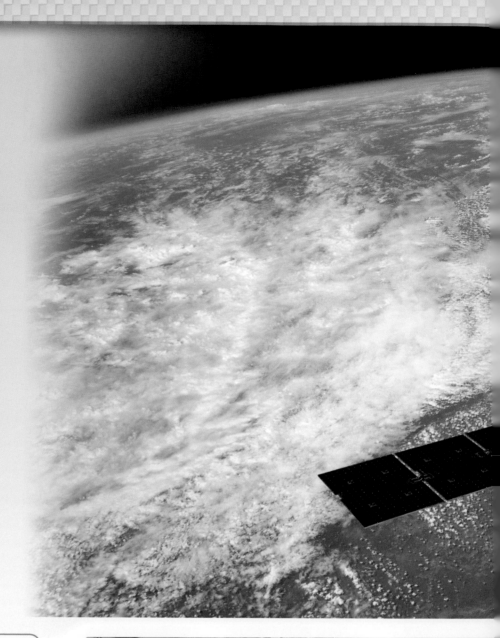

RIGHT..
THE SPACEX DRAGON TAKING CARGO
TO THE INTERNATIONAL SPACE STATION.

PRIVATE COMPANIES

The Commercial Orbital Transportation Services project was started in 2006, opening up a new world of private space travel. Rockets are developed, built, and flown by private companies, and NASA is just a customer.

As a result, costs for getting into space are coming down fast. SpaceX, the leading private space company, is developing a rocket called Falcon Heavy that can carry twice as much as Delta 4 for $100 million per launch, so that the cost per ton is $1.8 million: one-tenth as much as the U.S. government rocket!

RIGHT..
SPACEX STAFF SHOW HOW THE DRAGON
COULD BE ADAPTED TO CARRY CREW.

MOON EXPRESS

SpaceX is just one of several projects in development that aim to make private space travel a reality.

Moon Express wants to set up what it calls a "lunar railroad," a program of missions to the Moon that will start with robotic landers and probes. These will explore the Moon, looking for ice and precious minerals, and later a permanent human colony will be set up on the Moon.

A moon base could be a vital stepping stone for missions to Mars. Alternatively, Martian missions could start off from space stations orbiting the Earth. Bigelow Aerospace is planning to sell cheap, inflatable space stations to companies developing these plans.

BELOW..
INFLATABLE SPACE STATIONS COULD BE USED TO CREATE A BASE ON THE MOON.

DRAGONS AND GRASSHOPPERS

In 2012 SpaceX successfully made the first commercial resupply of the International Space Station (ISS) with its Dragon capsule, launched by Falcon 9 rockets. The Dragon capsule is reusable: after delivering its load of supplies it is filled up with equipment to bring back to Earth, and then splashes down in the ocean.

SpaceX is contracted to do eleven more supply missions to the ISS, and also intends to develop the Dragon capsule as a crewed module so it can be used to carry people into orbit and maybe beyond. SpaceX is also developing the Grasshopper rocket, a vertical takeoff and landing rocket stage that will make launch rockets reusable, so that they become even cheaper. As the cost of getting into orbit tumbles, it will be possible for everyone from private companies to universities and even schools to send satellites and experiments into orbit.

ORBITAL AIRSHIPS AND SPACE ELEVATORS

Other private companies are exploring revolutionary ways of getting into space that don't use rockets. JP Aerospace's Airship to Orbit plan involves using airships to lift heavy loads high into the atmosphere without needing expensive fuel. V-shaped flying wing airships will accelerate the loads into orbit.

Even more ambitious is the **space elevator** project, which would run a thin but extremely strong wire from an orbiting space station down to the surface of the earth. The wire would be used as an elevator cable, allowing capsules to run up and down, providing a permanent bridge into space.

SPACE TOURISM

Space is about to become a top vacation destination. There are at least six private companies battling to be the first to get tourists into outer space. Alongside these "spacelines," there are plans for space hotels, spaceports, and even travel insurance for astro-tourists.

In the future, the dream of flights into space will become routine and relatively cheap, with thousands of people experiencing the thrills of weightlessness and the joy of seeing the earth from space.

VISIT SPACE

Virgin Galactic's SpaceShipTwo is likely to be the first vessel to actually carry space tourists. Here's how the journey will work.

1 At an altitude of 9.1 miles (15.5 km), SpaceShipTwo launches from the mothership.

2 At 62 miles (100 km), SpaceShipTwo reaches the Kármán line, where passengers become astronauts.

3 Virgin Galactic's maximum planned altitude is 68.6 miles (110 km). SpaceShipTwo raises its wings after the rockets ignite.

4 Reentry into the atmosphere in the wing-raised ("feathered") position.

5 At 13.6 miles (21.5 km), SpaceShipTwo defeathers into glider mode.

6 SpaceShipTwo glides home.

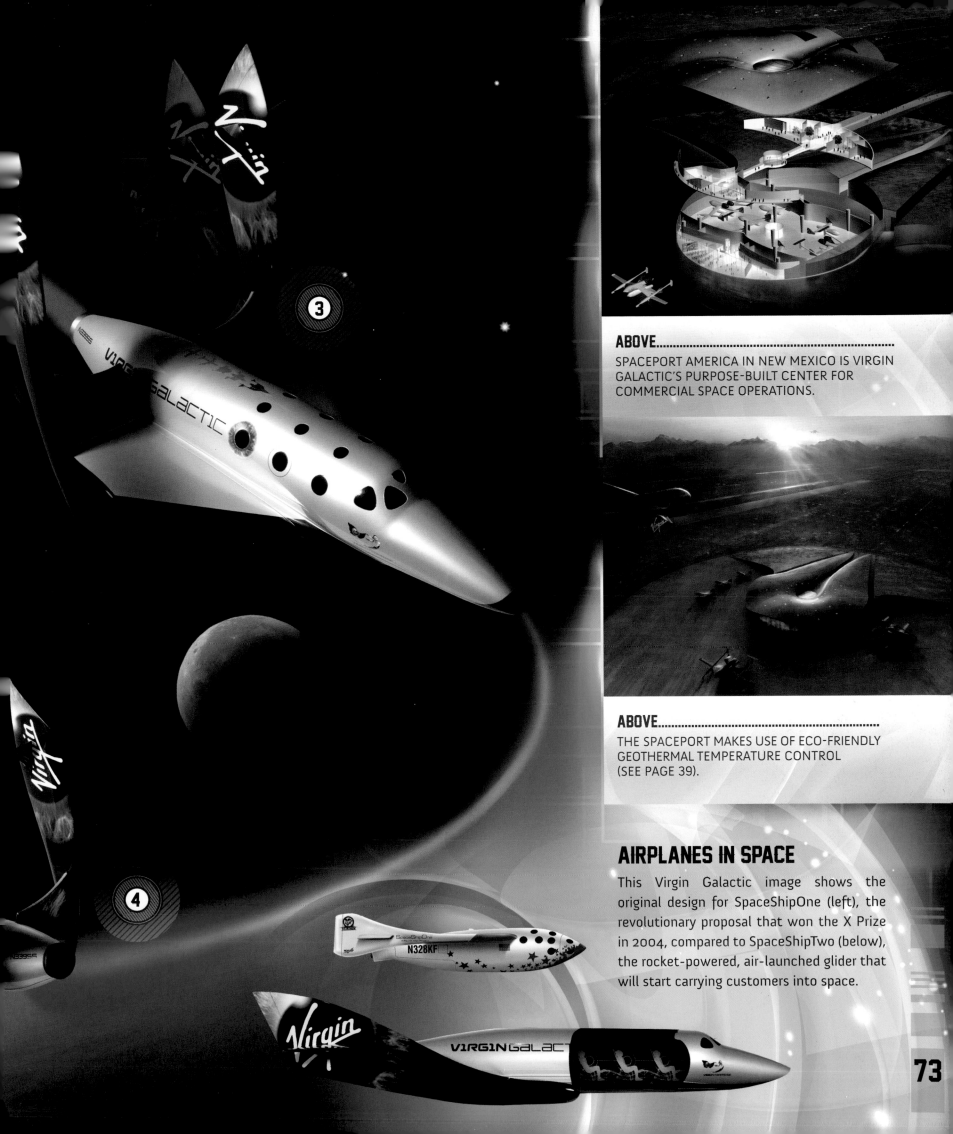

③

④

SPACEPORT AMERICA IN NEW MEXICO IS VIRGIN
GALACTIC'S PURPOSE-BUILT CENTER FOR
COMMERCIAL SPACE OPERATIONS.

ABOVE..

THE SPACEPORT MAKES USE OF ECO-FRIENDLY
GEOTHERMAL TEMPERATURE CONTROL
(SEE PAGE 39).

AIRPLANES IN SPACE

This Virgin Galactic image shows the
original design for SpaceShipOne (left), the
revolutionary proposal that won the X Prize
in 2004, compared to SpaceShipTwo (below),
the rocket-powered, air-launched glider that
will start carrying customers into space.

N328KF

Virgin

VIRGIN GALACTIC

73

TREASURE FROM OUTER SPACE
ASTEROID MINING

There could be a new gold rush ... in outer space! Some of the **asteroids** in our solar system contain vast mineral resources. Just one of these rocks might yield, for example, up to $3 trillion of platinum.

These staggering sums of money have inspired a group of adventurous millionaires to fund an ambitious new project called Planetary Resources, which is pioneering the concept of **asteroid mining**. Although their plan sounds like science fiction, it is based on solid fact.

It's possible that water could be extracted from asteroids out in space and pumped into rockets for fuel. Fuelling rockets out in space could save large amounts of money as launching rocket missions from Earth costs trillions of dollars.

FACTORIES IN SPACE

Research is underway to find a means of mining asteroids.

Swarms of small robots will dig trenches on the surface of an asteroid, sucking up chunks of rock and crushing them into powder. The ore will have to be melted and refined to produce minerals. This could involve gigantic space factories.

RIGHT.......................................
A COMPUTER SIMULATION OF ASTEROID MINING.

ABOVE..
THE FUEL HARVESTER CONCEPT BY DEEP SPACE INDUSTRIES.

BELOW..
THE FUEL HARVESTER PROCESSING PLANT.

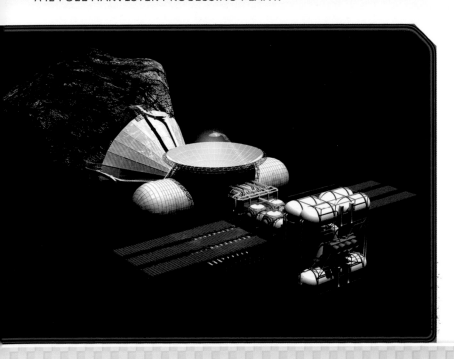

ASTEROID HUNTERS

The Planetary Resources plan is to launch a series of Arkyd 100 Leo satellites to hunt for suitable asteroids. The Leo space telescopes are revolutionary in terms of their low cost. Combined with the rapidly falling cost of getting into orbit, the Leo design will make it economically possible for a private company to put a fleet of space telescopes into orbit.

ABOVE...
AN ARKYD 100 LEO SATELLITE, TO BE
USED IN STUDYING NEOS.

NEAR-EARTH OBJECTS

Most asteroids in the solar system are in the asteroid belt between Mars and Jupiter. But for mining to be affordable, it is necessary to look at asteroids nearer to home: so-called near-Earth objects (NEOs).

A 2011 sky survey by NASA's WISE space telescope revealed that there are twice as many NEOs within easy reach of Earth than previously thought.

SUNKEN GOLD
MINING THE DEEP OCEAN BOTTOM

In 2012, filmmaker and adventurer James Cameron became only the third person, and the first since 1960, to visit the deepest part of the ocean: the bottom of the Marianas Trench in the Pacific.

Cameron had funded the development of the Deepsea Challenger, a vertical, torpedo-style sub with tall banks of super-bright LED lights on top of a tiny bubble of steel where the pilot sits. It's one of a new breed of underwater vehicles promising to open up the biggest, most mysterious part of our planet.

> CHALLENGER BEAT COMPETITION FROM THREE OTHER DEEP OCEAN SUBMERSIBLES, INCLUDING VIRGIN OCEANIC'S DEEPFLIGHT CHALLENGER, AND DEEPSEARCH, A SUB PARTLY FUNDED BY ONE OF THE FOUNDERS OF GOOGLE.

HOT SPOTS

We know more about the surface of the Moon than the bottom of the oceans, yet 71 percent of the surface of our planet is seafloor.

Some of the most valuable locations are where volcanic activity causes mineral-laden mud and superheated water to blast out of cracks in the ocean floor. Hydrothermal vents, or black smokers, feature water hotter than 212°F (100°C), crushing pressure, poisonous chemicals, and a lot of sea life.

RIGHT...

A BLACK SMOKER ON THE FLOOR OF THE PACIFIC.

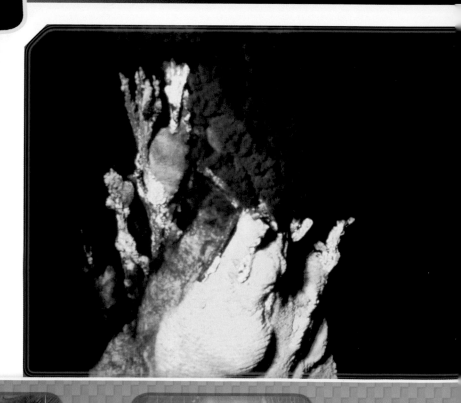

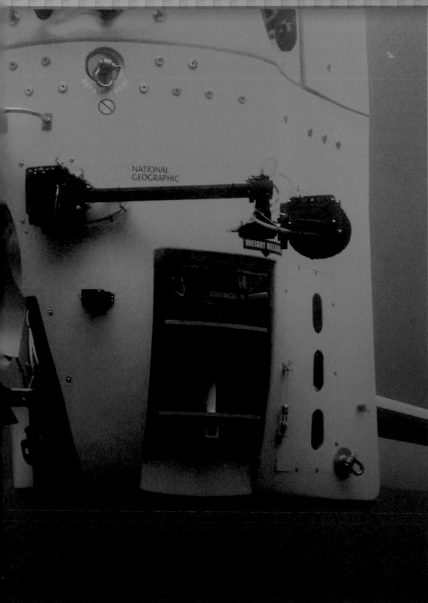

BOTTOM FEEDERS

Mining the ocean floor deposits will require trenching and cutting machines (robots equipped with mechanical diggers and rock-crushing teeth), which will "eat" chimneys and carve rock from the bottom, chewing it up into powdered rock. Suction devices could vacuum up the crushed rock, pumping it to barges on the surface for processing.

The Chinese are working on a nuclear-powered deep-sea mining station and mothership system that would work around the clock for months at a time.

BELOW..
ROBOTIC HARVESTING OF MINERAL
DEPOSITS FROM THE SEABED.

ABOVE..
THE DEEPSEA CHALLENGER HAS A VIEWPORT
FOR THE PILOT NEAR ITS BASE.

PROSPECTING THE OCEAN FLOOR

Mineral prospectors are very interested in the chimneys, or columns, of mineral-rich rock that form around hydrothermal vents. If these could be "harvested," trillions of dollars' worth of valuable minerals, including gold, could be available.

Several companies are working on deep ocean mining. Nautilus Minerals, for instance, is preparing to send teams of remotely operated submarines to identify the richest pickings.

POISONOUS HARVEST

Deep-sea mining could help prevent important mineral resources from running out, but would almost certainly cause great environmental damage. Hydrothermal vents are fragile and important ecosystems. Deep-sea mining would kick up clouds of toxic chemicals, while the barges at the surface would release floods of polluted water.

3-D PRINTING
BUILDING THE FUTURE

The way everyday objects are created is going to change over the next fifteen years. Everyone will have access to easy ways of turning their ideas into physical reality.

3-D PRINTING

Perhaps the greatest advance will be 3-D printing. At the moment a 3-D printer is a device that uses liquid plastic to print a 2-D layer, just like an inkjet printer. The plastic quickly sets hard, and then the printer prints another layer on top of it, building up layers until a three-dimensional product is formed.

But already there are printers that can use other materials, such as wood and metal, or that makes things with moving parts and electronic components. By 2025, you may not need to go to stores at all. You will simply choose a product online, hit "print," and your own personal version will be printed at home.

BELOW..............................

3-D PRINTERS LIKE THE MAKERBOT REPLICATOR ARE A HUGE HELP TO INDEPENDENT INVENTORS.